Majella

Guardian of Mothers

1726–1755
Born in Muro, Italy
Feast Day: October 16
Family Connection: Pregnant Mothers

Text by Barbara Yoffie
Illustrated by Katherine A. Borgatti

Liguori
ONE LIGUORI DRIVE
LIGUORI MO 63057-9999

Dedication

**To my family:
my parents Jim and Peg,
my husband Bill,
our son Sam and daughter-in-law Erin,
and our precious grandchildren
Ben, Lucas, and Andrew**

**To all the children I have had the privilege of
teaching throughout the years.**

Imprimi Potest:
Harry Grile, CSsR, Provincial
Denver Province, The Redemptorists

Published by Liguori Publications
Liguori, Missouri 63057

To order, visit Liguori.org or call 800-325-9521

p ISBN 978-0-7648-2293-3
e ISBN 978-0-7648-6912-9

Liguori Publications, a nonprofit corporation, is an apostolate of The
Redemptorists. To learn more about The Redemptorists, visit Redemptorists.com.

Printed in the United States of America
18 17 16 15 14 / 5 4 3 2 1
First Edition

Dear Parents and Teachers:

Saints and Me! is a series of children's books about saints, with six books in each set. The first set, *Saints of North America,* honors holy men and women who blessed and served the land we call home. The second set, *Saints of Christmas,* includes heavenly heroes who inspire us during Advent and Christmas and teach us to love the Infant Jesus.

Saints for Families introduces the virtuous lives of seven saints from different times and places who modeled God's love and charity within and for families. Saint Thérèse of Lisieux felt the love of her family and carried it into her religious community (which included her sisters). Saint Anthony of Padua is the patron of children, especially infants. Saint John Bosco cared for young, homeless boys, raising them like sons. Saint Thomas More, a father of four, imitated Christ's sacrificial love and devotion to the truth until death. Saints Joachim and Anne became the grandparents of Jesus, raising Mary as a sinless disciple. And Saint Gerard Majella, the patron of mothers, blessed families with food, knowledge, penances, and healing miracles.

Which saint stood up against a king? Who became a tailor and a lay brother? Which saint is "the little flower?" Who was known for his excellent preaching? Which saints lived before Jesus? Which saint climbed trees, did flips, and turned cartwheels? Find out in the *Saints for Families* set, part of the *Saints and Me!* series, and help children connect with the lives of saints.

Introduce your children or students to the *Saints and Me!* series as they:

—READ about the lives of the saints and are inspired by their stories.

—PRAY to the saints for their intercession.

—CELEBRATE the saints and relate to their lives.

John Bosco
1815–1888
Born: Becchi, Italy

Joachim and Anne
First century BC
Born: Nazareth (Joachim) Bethlehem (Anne)

Anthony of Padua
1195–1231
Born: Lisbon, Portugal

Gerard Majella
1726–1755
Born: Muro, Italy

Thérèse of Lisieux
1873–1897
Born: Alençon, France

Thomas More
1478–1535
Born: London, England

A long time ago, a special baby was born in the small town of Muro, Italy. His name was Gerard Majella. Gerard was a tiny baby. He was not very strong, and he was often sick. His parents loved him very much and took good care of him.

Gerard's father was a tailor who made clothes and suits for people. Gerard's mother took care of baby Gerard and his older sisters. She taught her children how to pray to Jesus and Mary.

As a child, Gerard went to church with his family. He liked to go to church. It was peaceful and quiet. Gerard liked to look at the beautiful statues and pictures. "I love you, Jesus. I love you, Mary," prayed Gerard.

When Gerard was twelve years old, his father died. He went to work for a tailor so he could help his family. Later he worked at the house of a bishop. Young Gerard learned many lessons. He learned how to be patient, obedient, and kind.

When Gerard was about twenty, he opened his own tailor shop. People liked Gerard. He was honest and fair. He gave money to his mother and to the poor. Gerard went to Mass every day.

One morning, he heard a sermon by a Redemptorist priest. "What a wonderful sermon! I want to join him and work for God," said Gerard. The priest tried to change Gerard's mind. "You should think and pray about this," he said.

"Oh, but I have prayed. Please let me go with you. Just give me a chance," begged Gerard. The kind priest said "yes." Gerard became a Redemptorist lay brother. Brothers do many things in the monastery. The work is hard, and Brother Gerard did not look very strong. But he did his work—and much more! First, he worked in the garden. Later he was a tailor and a cook. He liked to pray and work. Every day, Brother Gerard grew closer to God through prayer and penance.

When he was the doorkeeper at the monastery, Brother Gerard met many people. Some begged for food. "Take this food. I will pray for you," he said. There was always enough food to give to the hungry people.

Brother Gerard did whatever his superiors asked. He was obedient. Often he surprised them by knowing what to do before they told him. "How could this happen?" they asked. God had given Brother Gerard a special gift.

Sometimes the Redemptorist priests took Brother Gerard on missions to other towns. Brother Gerard enjoyed talking with people. He knew the secrets in their hearts. He helped people make good confessions. This was a special gift from God.

Many times, priests asked Brother Gerard questions about the faith. "Let me think a minute," he would say. His wonderful answers surprised everyone. God had given Brother Gerard the gifts of knowledge and wisdom.

Brother Gerard performed miracles. Miracles come from God. They help people believe in God. When Brother Gerard prayed for sick people, they got better. What a special gift from God!

When he prayed, he only saw and heard God. "Dear God, I love you and I trust you," prayed Brother Gerard. His faith was strong. He loved God with all his heart.

Holy Brother Gerard used his gifts to help others. After he died, people told stories about his life and many miracles. Today many people, especially mothers, pray to Saint Gerard and ask for his help.

Saint Gerard Majella was kind and helpful. He shared his gift of faith with others. Faith is a wonderful gift from God. How do you share your faith?

Put God at the center of all you do.
He will always be there to care for you!

Dear God,

you loved Saint Gerard

and blessed him with

many gifts.

he loved you with all

his heart and soul.

help me to love you.

show me how to do

your will.

Amen.

NEW WORDS (Glossary)

Lay brother: A member of a religious order who takes vows but is not a priest

Miracle: A wonderful event that cannot be explained and that shows God's love for us

Mission: Special talks given at a parish by a guest speaker

Monastery: The place where a religious order of men lives, prays, and works

Obedient: Doing what you are told

Penance: An act that shows you are sorry and helps you build good habits

Redemptorists: A religious order founded in 1732 by Saint Alphonsus Liguori

Superior: The head or leader of a religious order

Tailor: A person who makes and fixes clothing